Praise for *Hu...*

"[*Husbandry*], in its flow of couplets, c... poem, composed in chapters, but composed all in one rhythm, one spirit. One continuous breath—by turns tender, heartbroken, enraptured, delighted, angry, melancholy—all the turns of human family life. To look at those turns, to see them in granular detail, is not easy, but it's one way to let the light of the real be a kind of healing, if not a source of hope."
　　　　　　　　　　　　　　　　　　　—Jesse Nathan, *McSweeney's*

"*Husbandry*'s image-world has recalled for me what language really is and does in the deepest epochs of living. It is rare to encounter a genuine poetics of separation and single-parenthood, still rarer one which consecrates the drudgery and the glittering revelations of nurture from a position of candid interiority. Everyone is equal in this book, with the innocent justice life offers at the outset."
　　　　　　　　　　　　　　　—Rachel Cusk, author of *Second Place*

"In a clear, spare voice, *Husbandry* contemplates the joys and struggles of domestic life, detailing many luminous moments of fatherhood."
　　　　　　　　　　　　　　　　　—Marilyn Chin, author of *Sage*

"Joseph relegated to holy backdrop. Vader's chilling confession to a wounded Luke. Fathers undervalued, hastily drawn, overly romanticized, dismissed, dramatized, overlooked. Fathers called upon to be substitute everythings, then commanded to be less than shadows. Matthew Dickman's signature lyricism electrifies this new fractured phase of his life story, as a suddenly solo father who witnesses the visceral but tender unreeling of family, who must daily redefine his root as both father and son, and whose utterly stubborn love for his children reveals the chaotic, ungolden work of parenthood."
　　　　　　　　　　　　　—Patricia Smith, author of *Incendiary Art*

"Matthew Dickman's tenderly forensic, accomplished, and confronting book moves through bitterness to the domestic realities of the work of responsibility and love for our children. In the anxiety of being, nightmares have to be negotiated, and the role we play in showing a way through has to be scrutinized as we go. It's not easy, it never was, for any of us. And that's the gift of this book—though so specific, so personal, it can be for any of us."   —John Kinsella, author of *Insomnia*

"*Husbandry*—one of the most moving books of poems I have read—is told almost in a whisper that now and then breaks into a cry. Tough, plain, gorgeous, brave, innocent, full of dailiness, love, and heartbreak, these poems exist in that mysterious crossover place between the inner life and the lives of others." —Sarah Arvio, author of *Cry Back My Sea*

HUSBANDRY

HUSBANDRY

poems

MATTHEW DICKMAN

W. W. NORTON & COMPANY
Independent Publishers Since 1923

Excerpt from "Tidy," from *Exceptions and Melancholy* by Ralph Angel.
Copyright 2006 © Sarabande Books, Inc. Reprinted by permission.

For information about permission to reproduce selections from this book, write to
Permissions, W. W. Norton & Company, Inc., 500 Fifth Avenue, New York, NY 10110

For information about special discounts for bulk purchases, please contact
W. W. Norton Special Sales at specialsales@wwnorton.com or 800-233-4830

Manufacturing by Lakeside Book Company
Book design by Beth Steidle
Production manager: Beth Steidle

Library of Congress Cataloging-in-Publication Data

Names: Dickman, Matthew, author.
Title: Husbandry : poems / Matthew Dickman.
Description: First edition. | New York, NY : W. W. Norton & Company, Inc., [2022]
Identifiers: LCCN 2022019186 | ISBN 9781324021384 (cloth) | ISBN 9781324021391 (epub)
Subjects: LCGFT: Poetry.
Classification: LCC PS3604.I2988 H87 2022 | DDC 811/.6—dc23/eng/20220422
LC record available at https://lccn.loc.gov/2022019186

ISBN 978-1-324-07467-0 pbk.

W. W. Norton & Company, Inc., 500 Fifth Avenue, New York, N.Y. 10110
www.wwnorton.com

W. W. Norton & Company Ltd., 15 Carlisle Street, London W1D 3BS

1 2 3 4 5 6 7 8 9 0

You used to hold my hand
when the plane took off.
— SINÉAD O'CONNOR

I miss you too.
Something old is broken,

Nobody's in hell.
— RALPH ANGEL

My sister held me close and whispered to my bleeding head
You are the son of a mother fucker.
— THE PIXIES

CONTENTS

HUSBANDRY

In each of the stories
where children

are led out of their beds
at night by a broken

father or angry stepmother
and marched off

to be fed into the mouth
of a dark wood,

the children are supposed
to die. In some stories

they do. In others they
survive but must kill

a witch or an animal
in order to live

which is, to be fair,
a different kind

of death but a death all
the same. Imagine

the fog around their small
ankles like a shoreline

in the dark. Imagine
how cold their skin

would be beneath the thin
overcoats

of their nightshirts,
the little heat

the parents are giving
off beginning to dissipate

like dew as the children
take that last step

into the copse of trees
and are swallowed up.

There are so many ways
to eat the young.

Yesterday, Owen was riding
his red Radio-Flyer

tricycle around and around
our red dining room

table. Get me, poppa,
get me, you're a gob-a-lin,

come get me. And I know
I shouldn't have

really become a goblin,
that that was not what he was

asking for. He wanted his
poppa and a funny voice.

Instead my body grew
like a shadow and turned green,

craven and heavy.
You can't run from the gob-a-lin,

the gob-a-lin, the gob-a-lin,
I sang, and chased him

round the table, you
can't run from the gob-a-lin

I'm going to eat
your skin. Then he stopped,

knowing that I was
no longer there and looked

up at my face and not
seeing my face began to cry

and shake. I knelt down
and held him,

and said I'm sorry
it's just poppa,

was that too scary? We
won't play that anymore and he

calmed a little and said
I don't want him

poppa,
tell the gob-a-lin not to

come back. When you ask
parents how they ever raised

their children they will
often say

half the time I had no idea
what I was doing.

But I think we do know
what we are doing. And so does

the forest, and the dark
in the forest,

and the wind in the dark,
and the beasts,

the broken fathers, the angry
stepmothers,

the unconditional bond
become errant.

SPIDERS

When my youngest
wakes up

still inside
the nightmare

he is having
about spiders crawling

over his stomach
like ants

crawling over a very
soft and warm

piece of watermelon,
tunneling

in and out
of the watermelon,

I pick his wet body
up and hold him,

sing to him,
and in the flickering

of the hallway
I know it's really

me I'm holding,
like some ancient tool

from the bronze age
a mother had fashioned

to cook with or build
a house with.

I'm walking around
my apartment

crying into my own arms,
half asleep,

a pilgrim who, finding
the sacred artifact,

panics because he
doesn't know how,

now, he will ever
manage to get it home.

I carry my son and I
carry myself

and the dove of love
does something,

I forget, on a branch,
or in the light

of morning.
In the morning

the spiders have all
gone back to bed

inside my son's head.
His older brother

comes out to the living
room and sits

on the couch next
to us and asks

what happened last
night?

Your brother had a bad
dream, I say,

and then the little one
says yes, the spiders

came and said
bad things about us.

I don't have to
prove the spiders wrong,

just oh lord
give me and my boys

the memory
of what the dove

does or teach me how to be
the dove and not

the spiders though I love
the spiders more—

How quietly they work. How
they spin their worlds together.

CROSSING GUARD

I'm walking with Hamza
the year we met,

the year he turned six,
not long after

his five-year-old
friend died in a car

accident, sitting in
the backseat, wrapped

in a seatbelt, the
black strap across

his shoulder like
the yellow sashes kids

wear when called to be
crossing guards, but

this kid being too
small for the shoulder

part that his neck
ends up snapping

quick, just like that,
snap. The sound

of which must have
been swallowed up

by the impact
of the two cars, a small

sound in comparison,
as small as the boy

it came out of,
smaller to be sure

than the scream of
the mother as the cars

came together and smaller
still, than the scream

of the mother after.
Hamza and I are walking

beneath some maple trees,
the leaves

turning red and yellow,
brown and some

fallen to the ground
so that when we walk

we are making a kind
of swishing sound

together, like we were
wearing long gowns.

In front of us
someone has dragged

a dead squirrel off
the street and onto

the sidewalk, placed
some sticks over

the matted fur along
with a couple leaves.

Have you ever met
A dead person?

Hamza asks, sort of
at me but also

at the body
of the squirrel.

I have friends who
have died, I say.

Me too! he says. How
did your friends die?

We have stopped
walking and are instead

standing right in
front of the squirrel

and I can tell something
has eaten part

of its stomach. Well,
one of my friends

sat inside his car
while it filled up

with really poisonous
air and he died by breathing in

that air. Did all
your friends die like

that? he asked. No, I said,
just him. My other

friends died in other
ways. I have a friend

who died too, he
says. How did your friend

die? I ask. He got his
neck broken, Hamza says,

and then looks back down
at the dead animal

in front of us. I'm sorry,
I say.

For a moment I think
we will be standing

here forever, he and I,
watching death

do its slow work
like someone restoring

a painting
but in reverse. It had

begun to get dark
and Hamza reached up

to hold my hand. What
else do you like?

he asked, as if catching
a thread we had lost.

I like going to
the movies, I like eating

popcorn. Me too, he said,
I like popcorn most of all.

THE GIFT

When, during one
of our dreaded

nights
on the couch together

planning our escape
from one another

like starved sailors
on an island

where one wanted to stay
beneath the palm trees

and hold hands
and listen to the sea

even as they starved
and the other wanted

to leave, because for her
the unknown was always

better than the known,
she told me

that part of the reason
she wanted to

have a child, to have
one with me,

was that somewhere
inside she knew

she would leave
and wanted me

to have something once
she left. An animal

for me, a friend on the island,
someone to love

other than her. I think I said
"oh." I think I was supposed to

say thank you. Thank you
for this. As if

the child was a gift
wrapped in glittering paper

from the emissary
of twilight, a parting

gesture that was supposed
to make the parting

about kindness and not cruelty.
I said "oh"

but inside my body
I was walking through

the snow with Owen
in my arms

trying to cover
his face from the cold.

I was walking
through a forest

at night, holding
Owen's hand and ringing

a bell to find
his older brother.

What a strange gift,
I thought.

"Oh" I thought
and that "oh" meaning

oh of course who would
ever want to be

with me.
Children are

miracles, people say.
Children are

gifts, people say.
And about death

some say we are
food for worms, my love,

we are food for worms.
But I think

we are leftover
honey for raccoons.

I wanted you to have
something, she said,

and in that moment,
like Christ

turning the water,
spinning it with her long

fingers, into wine,
she miraculously

took everything
and gave everything too.

Sitting across from us, his back straight as a chair. His hands clenched like a jaw.

FATHER

In the un-story
of my life

I am three years old
and my father

lifts me
into the air

and then catches
me again and again,

pulling me into him.
Or

I am thirteen
years old and my father

sits on the porch
with his arm around

me and says yes, yes,
look, everything

will be fine, I'm here.
In the un-story

he has his ties
and pressed shirts

hanging in
the closet next to

my mother's blouses.
The smell of his

cologne washes over
everything like a pot roast

roasting all
Sunday. But in the story

of my life my father's
sons have to

call him again
and again and again

and again
like small children

hitting a drum
they can't stop hitting.

They have to beg
for his attention,

and one even dies,
in his way, for him,

and like life, is buried
without him.

In the story
of my life I inherit

the fathers
of other kids, other

sons. How lucky
am I?

Fathers with names
like Joseph,

Yosef, Josiah, Yasef,
meaning *he will add.*

Meaning he will
lift you up and catch you.

Meaning he will
sit with you, and your

sorrow will be his
too. Fathers with names

like Ernie, Ernest, Ernesto,
Arnošt, meaning *kindness.*

Meaning he will walk
among the lepers

of your actions
and listen to them.

Meaning he will not fail you
even as you fail yourself.

Right now dusk is moving
around the house

like a bad babysitter
waiting for her boyfriend

to come over, re-applying
her eyeliner. Outside

some coyotes are lighting
up the air like teenagers.

Meanwhile in the story
of my life

I lift my three-
year-old up into the air

and then catch
him but also catch

myself. In the story of
my life I put

my arm around
my thirteen-year-old

But also around
myself. When I feed

them I feed
myself. When I cool

a fevered forehead
with a cold

rag I cool my own
anger. When I leave

I also return to them
and return

to myself. I know
there are

really three children
in the story of my life.

I must make a home
for each of them.

LILAC

One look at the lilac, one smell
and my childhood is—

dogs scratching at the sliding
glass door, bits

of bottles coming up
like weeds in the grass,

a dirty towel
down by the foot

of the tree, Lysol cans, small
packets of Land O' Frost

turkey meat—
there in front of me in spring,

in the wonderfully fat rain,
flowering purple

and whatever
the pinkish purple is called

and the white ones too.
They smell like

my siblings, like
the backs of my infant

son's ears, like my son
who I would kill someone for.

Before he was born I wouldn't kill
anyone. But now I would.

And after I'd get a coffee
from Starbucks, a coffee and a piece

of that amazing lemon
frosted lemon cake

and think nothing of it,
and read the paper and hold him

against my chest
and listen to his body living,

alive outside
his mother's body, and the lilac

outside on the street, outside
everyone, and heavy in the rain.

CHORES

When their mother
left me I felt

like everyone says
they feel,

like I was going to
die every day

for years. But here
I am, alive

as any field of clover,
alive as any

balloon, though
the balloon has

been reshaped
into an animal

for a child, for
a child's happiness.

Alive as any memory
of an ocean

one might have,
the moon above and in

the ocean, alive,
even more alive

than Roman coins,
alive and old,

alive and young.
When their mother

came home those last
nights after being with

someone else, I felt
stupid and ashamed

and dying but
maybe, at least

she felt
alive, alive as any

goodbye, alive as
any monk covered

in kerosene. I
thought I would be

dead for a long time,
but look! I'm alive

and it's evening
and my sons and I

are all in our
beds after a long day

of doing our jobs
being alive.

Our three sets of arms,
of legs, of eyes,

our muscles all
different sizes and the

mostly soft life
of the penis, all asleep

or almost asleep.
The sound of the train

giving way to
the sound of a raccoon

moving through
the backyard looking

for something to
eat, a cat to kill.

In the morning, after
I make the boys'

breakfast, after I
sit drinking coffee,

watching them eat,
loving the sounds

their mouths make,
I will clean the house.

Sometimes I will be
on my knees,

and sometimes I will
be standing up.

PRIMITIVE

As for my mother
she only slapped me

once across the face
but hard enough

that I stumbled
back and couldn't

face her. Before
that and after

it was only wooden
mixing spoons

against my ass,
spoons whose real

job was to fold
batter in a bowl.

And sometimes a rogue
hanger but not often

and not just
anything at hand.

For instance she
never, in a rage, blindly

grabbed a rolling pin
to swing at me,

or a belt, for that
matter, she never pulled

a belt from a closet
to bear down on a cheek,

on any of the four
cheeks a child has.

And of course she did
not hit me, spank

me, scream or yell
at me more

than she ever did
not, her hands

so busy folding her
children's clothes,

cooking them dinner,
running their baths,

holding their hands,
lifting them into bed.

What had the most
horsepower in our house

was love and love's
experiment called grief.

As for me, I have
shamed my oldest son

in public and private,
I have buried his

body in the soil
of silence and watched,

almost happily, as he
coughed up the dirt.

I have wanted to
shake the youngest one

hard like you would
shake an apple tree

so that not only would
the ripe apples fall,

but also the apples
not yet ready.

To shake and shake
until no apples

were left in the arms
of the tree,

when he has gotten out
of bed the twentieth time,

but grab him instead
by the branch of his wrist

too hard, too much
like a father

who may not be
his father,

and yank him back
to bed

so I could return
to the nightly

business of being
angry at his mother

for leaving me. Go back
to the insomniac

hours I like to
collect like stamps.

When they are asleep
I go to each child

and kiss them on
their sweaty foreheads.

As for life it feels
too primitive,

too much blood and fur,
too humid and heaving

and growling. So much
so, that in the morning,

when I make the boys
pancakes, I'm afraid

they'll be able to taste it.
The iron. The tangy musk.

Olive seashells
in the air

you can eat.
The very inner of the inner ear

in the breeze.
Last night my son dreamt

about falling
out of trees.

I had almost forgotten
that we were simians.

The fiddlehead turns
on itself but only ever in love.

Green cinnamon roll,
a snake too small to hunt anyone.

Curled in like my son's
fingers, his fists.

More beautiful than
a spider fern,

spun-in island, moldy
tongue of a hippo,

the eye of the forest.
When my son wakes up

screaming
I don't pick him up

right away. I tell him where
he is and who I am.

At night all the fiddlehead
wants to do is sleep.

When I sleep
I dream about death adders curling

around his body,
all of us making the same sound.

On my lap, then hers. Back and forth. The rest
of our life like that, the rest of his.

When Owen was born
I was afraid,

like all new
fathers are afraid,

that I would drop
him and break

his head, still
shaped like a cone,

the shape his head
took so smartly

to slip out
of his mother's body

and pierce the world.
Soon I had endless

dreams where the sky
broke and the soul

of the sky slipped
out and moved like a giant

pink squid above
the back porch,

the street, the grass.
When I woke

I would go to him
and lift him up

and rock him and move
my fingers along

his new spine
like a harp. I had

what you would call
anxiety. I kept thinking

about what would happen
if I stepped on him,

on his head as he lay
on the wool

baby blanket,
how my foot would feel

coming down and through
him, his baby-skin,

his beginning-skull.
How the whole world

would turn into
a kaleidoscope coffin—

repeating forever.
I kept thinking

what would happen
if I forgot him

in the car, in the sun
while I walked

through the cool
air of some winding

grocery aisle,
how the plastic parts

of his car seat
would melt into him,

and him into it, how
his diaper would be

too full and too hot.
And I thought about all

those fathers
in the animal kingdom

who eat their young,
eat their hearts out

of their chests,
not because they are hungry,

or jealous, no,
not because of some ancient,

locked-in thread
of DNA that has yet to evolve,

but because they do not
know how to eat themselves,

which is what they really
want, to devour

the thing they hate
the most, the star-filled

wagon of the Self, that
bag of meat and bones

they did not ask to be.
I did not ask to be.

But here I am, in love,
cradling this hairless

human animal who comes
from a kingdom

of up-right ants
with fingers and toes.

And my only job now,
in all the world,

is to not destroy my kids,
and in turn,

teach them not
to destroy others,

even though, of course,
I will and they will,

locked-in as we are
and free as any other animal.

NATIVITY PLAY

When in the nativity
play my best friend

got to be Joseph
and my second best friend

got to play the Shepherd
and my third and fourth

and fifth best friends
all held the ancient

and sacred gifts of gold,
frankincense and myrrh,

while my role was invented,
the role of the "neighbor"

the nun said, who comes
to see the baby but doesn't

give or say anything,
I began to feel Herod's

blood in my eight-year-old
body and wanted them

all dead, my desire to be
chosen and my shame

at not being chosen
being so great, being

the only answer I could
come up with. Both then

and now. I have always
done what people have told

me to do, like a clothespin,
quietly. When my mother

said wash the floors
I got on my knees and washed.

When the adult
stranger at the playground

said give me your bicycle
I gave him my bicycle

and let him run his
fingers through my hair

and kiss me on my cheek
before riding off

through the grass. I stood
there saying nothing

and doing nothing. I would
have been a good Nazi,

I would have been a good
oak tree, I would have stood

very still while bugs
ate me. I wouldn't have even

moved one branch. Last
night my three-year-old

half woke from a nightmare
screaming "I don't

want to. I don't want to"
and I knelt down

and rubbed his sweaty
back and said "honey, you

don't have to, you don't
have to" until he quieted

and in his mind whatever
terrified him slipped away.

I was astonished.
I can't imagine,

even in a dream, yelling
at anybody or anything

and telling them I don't
want to, I don't

want to when all I would
be able to manage

would be ok, ok. You will
be the neighbor,

the nun said.
What does the neighbor

do, I asked? Nothing, she said
the neighbor does nothing.

PORPOISE

In the morning
my three-year-old

looks up from his
cold glass

of milk, the color
of a white dogwood

flower, and says
poppa, you have a penis

and I have a penis.
And I say yes

you have a penis
and I have a penis.

But I'm a princess
and you are not

a princess. And I
say yes, you are

a princess and I am
not a princess.

Outside the white
animal-shaped clouds

are pulsating
above the schoolyard.

I have an older brother
my son says

and I say yes you do.
You have an older

brother too, poppa.
Yes, I have an older

brother too but he is
dead. Now one of the clouds

is opening its mouth
like an exhausted lion.

My son wants to ask me
how he died

but instead he says
how did he get dead?

I love this question.
To get something

is to receive something.
It is the opposite of loss.

It is the act of gaining,
of having something

given. And so my older brother
wasn't taken by death

but acquired it,
collected and sustained it.

Now one of the clouds
is moving toward another

like an adult toward
a child who is not theirs.

He was sad is what I tell
my son, he was sad

and he got dead on purpose.
Poppa, you get sad

and I get sad but we have
popsicles too.

Yes, I say, we have
popsicles too.

And porpoises poppa,
we have porpoises.

Sometimes our mornings
together stretch out

like an eternal
current, like a cloud.

In the yard the dogwood
burns out in the sun.

It just stands there while
the sun subsumes it.

LAUNDRY

At first I folded
her clothes and Hamza's

clothes until
eventually he became

my son and folding
his small shirts

or his mom's black jeans
meant I was folding

my new family, folding
love and the heat

of love quivering
from the socks

and T-shirts. Then
we had a baby

and I folded his
even smaller clothes.

I was on my knees
for love, organizing

it by size and color.
I was kneeling

in the fabric-softened
chapel of love

and when I would rise
to put everyone's clothes

away I could hear
a lost bell

inside me ringing,
each article of clothing

an accounting
of devotion:

Spin-cycle devotion.
Detergent devotion.

Lint and the comfort
of cotton devotion.

I folded as a practice,
an exercise,

and when, eventually,
she was somewhere

in the dark
with another person,

removing the clothes
I had just folded

yesterday, I was at home,
on the floor,

making sure that when
she got home

her clothes were ready,
and placed them

next to mine, though the
piles no longer belonged

alongside one another.
I wanted so much

to only ever fold her
clothes,

so devoted to making
sure the seams matched,

the wrinkles
smoothed out.

I was folding for
no one, for everyone.

I was like the branch
of an elm tree, broken

off and lying
on the ground in the rain,

still blooming, still
thinking it was part

of the tree and never
dreaming that

a dog or a stranger
would eventually

carry it away— toward
what, I cannot tell you.

BLUEBELLS

Blue light ringing through
the green grass.

The bent heads of petals
are not praying

to anything or anyone.
Only we are

standing in a field of them,
my son and me and me

holding him.
In my arms he stretches

out to the very far ends of the earth
like a radio signal

made of skin and organs,
of everything.

I was singing a song to him
I made up

about rabbits.
Since yesterday morning

he has not been
crying as much as screaming

like it is terrifying
to wake up.

It is terrifying to wake up
and terrifying to sleep

and his feet going blue in the cold
spring air

in which he is growing.
His mother is growing him

with the milk she makes
all day,

the song I am singing to him
puts him to sleep,

will put me to sleep,
very much like a voice

calling from far away.
The words of which you can't

quite make out. You
could be hearing

the ocean, you could be
hearing the freeway.

Whatever the voice might
or might not be

the truth is that you
will never know if it is

hurting or
hungry or nothing at all.

I know what I'm
supposed to say

after the schism,
the separation, the breakup,

after all her things
except for

the smell of her,
except for

the children,
are packed up

and driven away,
when on the phone

a friend's voice,
like peonies

thrown up into
the air, says

well you know
Owen would never

have been born,
and Hamza,

you would never
have known Hamza—

I am supposed to
say yes, yes,

I would never
take it back,

my life, blindfolded
caretaker,

as if the children
were a stay

of execution,
as if the children

were an antidote
ground

into powder
and stirred into

a glass of orange
juice. I am

supposed to say
they are worth it,

all the pain,
the morphine

drip of meanness,
year after year.

But some nights,
I must tell you,

arriving like big
iron ships

of darkness into
the harbor

of darkness,
I think no, they are

not worth it,
that is, I wouldn't know

in a life without
them.

It would be a bit
like walking

beneath
a bird-less sky,

happy and whistling
in a world

where birds never
existed, not one wing.

I would only be
a father to myself

and have no idea
how it would feel

to lift Owen
into the air

or change his diaper
and love the smell

of his urine, or
what it means to have

Hamza shaken
by some teenage

loss suddenly sit
next to me on the couch.

I wouldn't have
all these dishes

to do or sandwiches
to make,

or Band-Aids to place
on barely bleeding

knees or pizza parties
to throw.

I wouldn't have
toys to pick up,

or the death
of children to worry

about, I wouldn't
have more than one

toothbrush standing up
in its tin cup,

or screen-time
to manage or bicycles

to buy or birthdays
to plan or hair to cut

or time to measure
with a broken pencil

along the doorjamb
of the kitchen

where I mark the inches
as the boys

outgrow being boys,
I wouldn't have,

I wouldn't have known
the difference, I wouldn't.

STROKE

The hotel sign blinking
in the brain

of my body
stops blinking but not

the whole sign,
you know, just a couple

of the letters,
the H and T.

The E and L
so all that is left

when the whole left
side of my body

comes to an end
is the O.

I am sitting across
from a young

writer, drinking coffee
and she is asking

me what I did.
What were you doing

when you were
in your twenties

she asks. And I am
saying something like

trying to write
a lot of poems

but the words
come out all slurred,

they come out
like pushing your tongue

through a clay door,
the word poem

becoming *proroom*.
And then any control

I had had over
my body

floats up and out,
really it flies, it leaps

off the ledge of me
and I remember

while falling
from my chair

to the ground, trying
to apologize.

The half of my brain
that was still

alive, as alive as
a deer

standing in a meadow
in the morning

licking dew off
the blades of grass,

telling what was left
of me that I was just

tired. You're just tired
the left side

of my brain said,
you're just tired,

this is normal.
The normal not normal

blood clot
in the right side of my brain

wiping everything
away like a teacher

wiping chalk away
with an eraser,

the blackboard
full of sines and co-sines

and then just long
strokes of white,

a white field in winter,
a white sky

before rain. A white
sheet of paper.

Through the tunnel
of my body

I could hear someone
ask me are you ok?

My whole life someone
asking me

are you ok,
are you feeling well?

I'm just tired
I thought.

And then this
thought: I'm not.

A hand on the hand
I could still feel.

They are coming
the voice said,

it's ok, you will be ok.
The sound then

of the ambulance
from far off.

The sirens getting
closer, lights

and sirens approaching
my body

from a street far off.
That's something

I never thought of
before.

That sirens are always
approaching

a body, that's the whole
reason for them

to let everyone know
there is a body.

I thought of my son
at home,

seventeen months old,
pointing to the window

in the living room,
saying

siren siren siren
and up up up.

I was lifted up
onto the gurney,

my shirt cut off
in the ambulance,

and arriving
at the hospital

the triage nurse
asking

are you Matthew Dickman?
Yes. Up up up

I thought.
Death is not a design,

not an idea.
Death is the body I know

this now, it's your arms
and legs,

your whole
cardiovascular system.

It is the whole of us
only we walk around

enough to think
it isn't.

The blood clot is doing
its job,

it's doing exactly what
it was made to do

and the only thing you
need to do

when you are dying
is to die.

Nothing else.
You don't need to

fold the laundry
or clean

the kitchen floor,
you don't have to

pick your children up
from school.

Unlike
the rest of your life,

there is only this one
thing. You don't even

have to be good at it
you just have to

do it. A list of chores
with just one

chore. In the operating
room I'm awake,

made to stay awake,
while the surgeon

threads a "line"
through the artery

in my groin
and up through all

the rooms, through
the room of my legs,

and the room
of my chest,

through the room
of my neck

and into the room
of my brain.

When I put my son
to bed I give him

a bottle of milk,
and rock him and sing

it's time to rest your body
it's time to rest

your mind,
it's time, oh it's time

to rest your brain.
The surgeon is able

to grab the clot
and slip it through

and out of all the rooms,
into the one he's working in.

I can hear everyone
in the operating room clapping,

because they are happy,
because it took

that one try
to get it all, to remove

the clot and then
the left side of me

begins to move again,
and there it is,

I have to pee,
my body is done

with this death.
And now there is nothing

to do but wait
for the next death.

I have never been more
inside than that

moment. I have never
wanted anything

as much as I wanted
to stand up

in that room
and walk out through

the automatic doors
to you— you, Julia,

to walk right into your arms
like walking into the world itself.

His face lit up by the screen in his hand, illuminated like a new species in search of a name.

For weeks after
the separation really

kind people kept
telling me that I was

on a journey, this is
your journey

they would say
and I would want to

scoop out their
eyeballs with one

of my grandmother's
silver grapefruit

spoons. Scoop them
out and eat them

and say, with my mouth
full, this is what

I think of journeys.
My mother's childhood

had horses in it. My
father's childhood had

mean mothers in it,
grand and not. My childhood

had fathers in it
but it was as if their

kids were watching them
through telescopes

from a safe distance,
a bluff above the sea

of whiskey and eggs.
For the first two months

of Owen's life,
he and I slept together

on the floor
of the living room

so his mother could sleep
without us,

so she could rest and heal
and dream.

When he was hungry
I would deliver him

into her sleeping arms
like an envelope

containing a truce
of some kind,

delivered to a king
who bled each night

of the new war. For
the first six years

of Hamza's life he did
not know me

and there was nothing
I could have done

for him. It's fall
again and I am

looking at the family
raking leaves

together across the
street and thinking

I really wanted to have
a family. Loss has

a peculiar way of
making us feel more

important than we are.
Half-gods crying

and fucking our way
out of the simple

truth that we are
not special.

I am not on a journey,
I am cooking

dinner for my kids.
I am washing their

hair and underwear,
I am trying to go

for walks outside,
trying to eat more vegetables.

If my children do
not bathe for a few days

they begin to smell
like pond water.

It's all I can do
not to fill my pockets

up with stones and wade out
into the middle of them.

HUSBANDRY

Both of my sons are laughing
at and with each other,

laughing the way something wild
does, with every part of

its pelt, blood, teeth,
and genitals. I am walking

around the apartment
being afraid of myself.

I'm not so much afraid that I will
collapse as I'm afraid I am the collapse,

I am the falling apart and hard to
keep it together.

I have to keep it together. I have to not
pass out all over them.

* * *

Owen sleeps so still, so
quiet with his stuffies,

I can't manage to fall asleep
without wondering if

he's dead, without
getting up every half

hour to check his breathing.
Is he breathing

or has he been eaten by
a pool of spiders,

a lake of ants, eaten
by beetles, swarmed

by wasps, if he is still alive
and if I touch him does he still move?

* * *

Hamza and I compare scars,
cuts, bruises.

He shows me where the door
closed on his

finger and how the finger is
like a red popsicle.

I show him the bottom of my foot
where the wine glass

went through and through
and all the way

to the top
but not through the top.

Scrapes, that's all, until the world
really does cut us into ribbons.

* * *

I wanted to be a husband.
Someone worth

being kept by another,
greater, animal.

I wanted to bring groceries home
and hear someone say

he's home! To be chosen.
I wanted to feel the cold heaviness

of a ring on my finger
and have it glow in the dark.

Have that ring cry out
that I was part of something beautiful.

For someone to stand next to me.
And in the standing, feel proud.

*   *   *

In my dream about the children
they are covered in fur,

they are walking on all fours around
the apartment, in the light

of the apartment. Hunting.
I'm so proud

that I know their names
and put out porcelain

plates with the food they like best
cut into fun shapes for them.

The children sniff and mew, they yap
and circle.

Sometimes I walk around all day
and I'm happy.

Major Jackson and I
are fond of drinking

dark beer and talking
about fathers, of his

who would leave and
return, leave and

return like a season
wearing a nightshirt

made out of fall
leaves and woodsmoke,

of mine who no one
can say left as he was

never really there,
a dream someone has

about money
though when they wake

there is nothing but
a penny's worth of light

on the pillow next to
them. When the ghosts of our

fathers ask us
to set the table we set

the table but no matter
how we fold

the napkins they are
always unhappy.

When the bodies
of our fathers ask our

bodies to be theirs
we set ours on fire.

Now our own sons
are staring

us down like bear cubs
staring down

a darkness from a forest
that only exists

for them. Now we are
inventing it as we go.

We have experimented
with holding their hands

and hugging them.
Sitting on the couch

with them. We are
trying to make sure

their feelings don't
turn into baseball bats

or guns or the unmade
bed of an inpatient's

medicinal ozone. Before
we were the fathers

of sons we were just sons
trying to survive our fathers,

flying down a hill inside
a blue Jetta

with a Blaupunkt cassette
player. And when our sadness

threatened to flood
the whole car,

Major turned up
The Roots so that whatever

darkness he and I
thought we were heading

toward lifted
and a kind of light

pulled up into the driveways
of our minds

like a father returned
home

from a business trip
he should never have made.

My children can't
get enough milk.

The teenager eats
bowl after bowl

of cereal, morning
and night, the honey

O's floating in
the white, turning

the milk sweet.
The three-

year-old drinking
glass after glass

but only in his
ladybug glass.

The milk is like
a liquid battery

I replace, carton
after carton,

cow or goat, nut
milk making

a kind of bloom
when I pour it

into my coffee.
It is a reminder

that everything
I give them

is manufactured.
A form that only

echoes the sacred
original, all

that I give is
made-up, all

but, I suppose,
my life,

which half the time
is kept warm

inside a slender
bottle of sleep,

my life which is
more water

than milk, my body
more tongue

than anything
else. If I could

I would nurse them,
I would turn

myself into
a bowl of cold milk

and call to them:
Here, little kitties,

here. Here is what
I have for you,

almost nothing,
but enough

that you don't starve.
Peanut butter

and jelly sandwiches,
macaroni and cheese,

some old carrots
and an apple, leftovers

spinning slowly on a carousel
in the microwave.

GIGANTIC

When my thirteen-year-
old looks up

from the blue
Pacific seabed

of his thirteen-year-
old life

and sees me standing
there like some bored

kid from a small
town full

of absent adults,
just standing

and staring off,
he asks

what are you
looking at?

Nothing, I say.
And that's true.

I'm not looking at
anything.

I'm looking for
something. Looking

for his mother, who now
lives across town.

His mother
who took

all her clothes
from our closet

and drove them to
a new closet,

a new house.
That day the hangers

she left behind
began to float.

I felt so bad
for them. That they

had had a whole
life with her

button-up shirts,
two black dresses,

her jean jackets,
slacks,

her winter coat and one
light, cotton bathrobe.

And now the hangers
had nothing.

The whole house felt
weightless, felt like

a wedding gown
floating alone in a river.

I think it's weird
that you're looking

at nothing, my son
says, and this time

he's right. His mother
no longer loves me

and I'm looking
at nothing.

And so I look at him,
who is two feet

taller than when we
first met, his bangs

flopping to one side.
It is so clear to me now

I almost can't believe
it: that to love

something completely
you don't have to

create it. You only
have to raise it.

Flowers and pets, snakes,
cats and dogs,

horses, ferns, children.
Outside, the rim

of the sky looks
so coarse, like sandpaper

and my son coughs.
Let me make you a snack

I say, and he says
make me a gigantic snack

and so I walk
into the kitchen

and look for something
that he will eat,

something that might
taste like love.

The clouds and rain and air
gather around the small grave he digs for the lavender.

Owen keeps asking what
happens to his body

when he dies, what happens
inside the body,

and I tell him
all your organs slow

down, your lungs and
heart, your liver,

and the blood in your
body stops moving

around your body, until
everything stops

and becomes quiet and
rests. He wants to know

if it's the same thing
for birds and when birds

die what happens to their
feathers, if the feathers

stay up in the sky and what
is a wolf, he wants

to know, and can it eat us.
He says that some things

come back after they die
but we don't want

them to. No, I say,
sometimes that's all

we want, no matter what.
For someone

we loved to come back
no matter how terrible

or painful it might
be. His older brother,

Hamza, is alone in his room
again, lying very still

on his bed working out
the compass of being

a teenager on his
Nintendo. I want to

take both boys out
into the yard and have

them bathe their feet
in the October grass.

Pull the cold air over
them like a woolen overcoat.

But I need to get dinner
going and I need to

grab the clothes from
the dryer and fold

them. I don't know what
we are going to eat

tonight. I don't know
how I will get the house

cleaned up before it's
time for bed. Before

I became a father my
greatest fear was dying

in a plane crash, the
plane stalling through

a cloud of birds. Now
I sit at the kitchen table

and stare and stare
at the gas bill

like looking out
the window at a car

on fire. Sometimes
I want to be a ghost

or a vampire, a zombie
slowly walking over a hill,

hungry for something
it can't name but,

with arms outstretched,
begs for anyway.

IN SERVICE

I must have begun
to hate

my body when I
learned that

it was not as good
as other people's bodies.

My adult body
is soft and changes

shape depending
on if I'm happy

or suffering.
I haven't taken

my shirt off
in public for years,

so it feels like
snow softly

falling into a field
of snow,

when I take a bath
with my toddler,

who's own body
hasn't yet been compared

to anyone or anything
but its own

life. My son who
says, while I'm drying

off from the bath, poppa,
are you drying

off your body? Yes,
I say, I am drying

off my body. I like
your body, poppa,

he says, and in
that moment I am not

ashamed of myself,
of the stomach

spanning out like
a milky manta ray.

When I first met
his mother,

she said you are not
the type of person

I usually date.
And I knew what she

meant since I had
met some of the other

men, who could walk
into a department store

and buy a pair of jeans
or a T-shirt

without ever trying
them on. I knew

she meant that my body
was something

to be tiptoed around
like a drunk

father asleep
on the davenport.

You might love him
but you wouldn't

want to wake him.
I'm getting dressed

while my son plays
with his foam

bath blocks. I put
on a pair of

black boxer shorts
and he looks up

at me and says
you look cool, poppa.

Then I begin to
put on a T-shirt

and he stops me.
Don't do that,

or I can't see
your belly. The sun

is flickering
through the small

window above
the bathtub and my son

and I are both in
out-of-body time

and in-body time.
Bodies are buried

in the ground
and what's left of

people after they
die is buried in the bodies.

We have the same
bodies, my son says,

which means we have
similar tastes, right

poppa? Right, I say.
so here is my

question: If I hate
my body

then don't I hate
his body?

Sometimes I want
so much

for mine to disappear
but not enough

that his would too. For
I am in service

to him as the snow
is in service

to the field and the stone
in the field

is in service to
the window

and the window is
in service

to the body
standing there, looking

out at the field,
wishing it were the sea.

TOMORROW

The first time I had
sex after my children's

mother had moved out
was with a woman

I barely knew who had
come to visit me like a

neurosurgeon arriving
in a cab at a country hospital

to visit a patient
whose time was running

out. Who sat next to
the patient with

a clipboard and said,
quietly, in the low

glow of the room,
the doctors here don't

know what they are
doing but don't worry,

everything will be ok,
you will see, you will

get better soon.
There won't even be

a scar. The rudder
of her tailbone

moved back and forth
through the water

and beneath
the water, the blue

sheets my ex
and I had bought together.

And beneath the blue
sheets the mattress

which still had the blood
of our son's birth

on it in the shape
of a parchment that had

burned around the edges.
I wanted to cum

but had to close my eyes
halfway in the half-dark

and pretend the person
with me was the person

who had left. Later
I remembered how I would

do that in a different
way with my friend Jason,

who, if it was dark enough
and we had been drinking,

and if we were hugging,
I could squint and turn

my head in this way
where he would look exactly

like my dead older
brother and how I would

hold the hug a little
too long, long enough

for Jason to pull away.
If I wanted to honor every ghost

in my life I would be
bowing all day.

I would be on my knees
like the forests

in California, burning
wildly and not

caring about who
or what I destroyed.

So consumed as I am
with my own life, rocking

back and forth
like a cantor singing

I want you, I want you,
I want you, I want you, I want.

RHODODENDRON

I'm walking my infant
son through a stand of rhododendrons.

It feels like we are walking
through a cloud of jellyfish

made of pink and purple paper
petals falling

to the ground.
These jellyfish are the fish of spring.

He is making sounds
like a mouse, small but all out

of his body. Inside,
his organs are so new

that they are both organs
and the beginnings of organs.

When he cries for his mother
to nurse him

he sounds like a rooster.
He is not

just hungry,
but hunger itself.

He is the thing
he cries for. Sunlight is turning

the rhododendrons
into balls of pink light if light

were liquid
and something else,

splashing,
that's what the pink is doing,

splashing all over us,
lucky without god,

animals under the bright pink
idea of earth.

A GHOST HOUSE FOR BUNNIES IN
DARKEST BEDTIME

My son and I are
building a house for us

to live in the rest of our lives
the rest of this morning.

He has placed all his stuffed
bunnies in a row.

Not sad, he says, they are
not sad.

They are ghosts
and smell like him,

like the ghost
of his urine and the ghost

of his drool.
We are stacking

the colorful blocks carefully
so they won't fall over

unless we make
the falling happen on purpose,

unless we destroy the very
home we seemed

to be born to build
together.

I'm jealous of his mother,
that he lived inside

her. Sometimes I wish
I could open myself up

and place him inside,
wrap him up

like wrapping him up
in a warm towel

for darkest bedtime,
for bunnies that smell

like grass,
mint, soil, and worms.

ANNIVERSARY

The night isn't as long
a year later, or bullied or rootless or night at all.

You need to do
something for yourself

is what she used to
say to me

while I stood washing
the dishes or folding

the children's pile
of warm clothes.

Now I believe that
she was talking

to herself like a knight
staring off over

the hay roofs of
some unimportant village

into the doors of a
dark and unknown

castle, saying I'm meant
for more than this.

I don't understand
why bravery

so often comes with
cruelty. I would be happy

staring at my kids
all day. I would be happy

watching snow fall
onto the green glass

of a greenhouse
until the glass broke

and the tomatoes inside
froze hard as baseballs.

My mother tells a story
about bringing her

sons to the mall when
we were eight

and says I saw how
people looked at you

and your brother, you
were such beautiful

children I was worried
something would

happen to you. I only
remember her looking

at us, saying I could have
looked at you all day.

The last time I talked
to my father

was the night of
my older brother's

cremation. He was sitting
on a couch staring

into an empty fireplace.
I hadn't seen him

for years but just
then I wanted to sit next

to him like you would
a child you found

lost in the mall,
and say it's ok, let's

find your parents, they
must be here somewhere.

I think I said, Allen,
I'm sorry Darin is gone.

And he made a sound
like a child might make

when reaching up for
a mother's hand

only to realize that it's not their
mother. He sighed

and said it's so strange
not having a son anymore.

And my father was right,
his son was dead

and gone and that
was the beginning and

the end of any story
I might ever tell

about love. Yesterday,
going to the store

to buy nighttime diapers
for Owen, I found myself

so happy that everyone
had to wear masks.

That I didn't have to
look at anyone's face.

That I didn't have to
look at mine. I watched

as boxes of different
kinds of cereal glided

by, watched cans
of vegetables become

cans of fruit. The music
playing in my head

was so beautiful
it was like the sound

my children's mother
made when she used to

walk through our house
in her socks.

PRACTICING

It is clear to me
now that the first

two years were
spent practicing

for the last six
months of us

being an us.
The amount of time

we spent breaking
up and coming

back together
like addicts

planning to get
clean and so taking

anything we had,
taking all of it.

Thrilled to be ruined,
knowing that

tomorrow we would,
hand in hand,

walk through some
golden gate

of sobriety. Over
and over,

tearful night
after tearful night,

we invented who
we would be to one

another, which was
everything

and nothing.
One of us would walk

away, just far
enough to feel like

they were dying
and then come falling

back like a Cold War
satellite falling to earth.

Each new apartment
we moved into

was practice, each
country, each trip

to the grocery store.
Each time she came or I came,

practice, and yes,
our children

too. No.
More than practice.

I think our children
were more than

that. Belonging more
to our fear

of finally leaving each
other for good

and not having
a reason to return.

So they became
a kind of cistern

where she and I could
store the water

of our sorrows. For
all the practicing

I never got good at it.
Not like her. She was,

in the end,
like an Olympic athlete.

The way she kept her
focus. The way she

thought of nothing
else and no one else

but for the finish
line, her form, beating

her best time. Maybe
even beating time itself.

I practiced and failed
but I was still breathing,

still alive enough
to try and stand

at the finish line
waving a flag

with her name on it,
and yelling her name,

I loved her so,
like a hometown crowd—

thousands of people on
their feet, all cheering for one.

GOODNESS

Crows are in the treetops
and so is the lilac sky

and so is part of a cloud
and so is spring and so are

the stomachs of the crows
and the intestines

and the brains and the
glistening feathers

of the crows which are more
dreamy than gory.

My kids are at their mother's
apartment and for a moment I don't

remember her name
and the feeling of that is more

dreamy than gory, more a feeling
of goodness

like staring down
at a rug you have just vacuumed

and seeing how
beautiful the threads of the rug are.

I sit at the kitchen table
with my back to the big window

and the big sun
and the children of other people

playing at the park across
the street. I'm addicted

to spring, to animals
I will never see

outside a zoo:
ocelots and gorillas, giraffes

and penguins. At dinner
last night my youngest

was digging small holes in his
baked potato and making

the stomach of the potato,
the intestines of the potato

into a little bowl and he
looked up at me and said

poppa your blood is
having a pool party.

I wanted to throw his potato
against the wall, he was so right.

Everyone is hurt
even people who have been really

shitty to other people.
Like me.

In my dream of spring
I have never hurt anyone.

I'm like a soft lamb
on a green hill which is,

I might add,
a gory thought.

It's the kind of thought that thinks
if I die there will be no more

ocelots or blades of grass
or rain showers or

worms coming up
out of the sidewalks

after the rain or children or spring.
The goodness of spring

isn't that we are
reborn but that we never

had to be
born in the first place.

RETURNING

On the days the children
are with their mother

the weight of them
somehow lightens and

expands. Wait, I think,
don't go is what

I feel, though I know
they will be returning.

Though I know they
are loved by her.

I walk around the two-
bedroom palace

I have made for the three
of us and lift their

dirty clothes into
my arms and cradle them.

I gather
all my children's

dirty clothes around me,
fanning them out

like a gown, and wait
for them to come home.

The smell of them rising
up from the pleats

of the gown, the sounds
of them still hanging

in the steam from the pasta.
I am their Lady in Waiting

and cannot wait to
dress them again, to feed

and bathe them, to hold
them and smell their skin,

but especially to feed them.
That most of all.

I pet the paws of stuffed
animals and say don't

worry, they will be home
soon. Why is everything

such a death? Death
is a gradient, a going away

and a coming back. Death,
a bee, a fat one, alone,

and lost in winter.
Fuck death. Give me

life, even the one
I have had with all

its stupid troubles, with
all its waiting around

for love, with all
its ignoring love, and

with all its mistaking
meanness for love. Give me

a sink full of dirty dishes,
give me a cup of coffee,

give me my children,
their sticky hands and feet,

and finally, give me a first kiss
that is also the last.

ACKNOWLEDGMENTS

Grateful acknowledgment is made to the editors of the following publications in which some of these poems have appeared in earlier drafts: the *American Poetry Review*, *The New Yorker*, *Poetry London*, *Poetry* magazine, and *Rattle*.

The poem "Stroke" was the recipient of the 2019 Rattle Poetry Prize, which helped sustain my family and me in a big way.

I'm honored to have the support of amazing friends including Carl Adamshick, Alex Behr, Michelle Bitting, Michael Bohrer-Clancy, Jessica Brown and family, Lucy Collier, Trinie Dalton, Tim Delany, Jason Dodge and family, Rosie Hart, Grace Hughes, Stephen Hitchcock, Hope and the folks at Greater Trumps bar, John Kinsella, Fergus Kinnell, Thomas Lauderdale, Matthew Lippman, Joseph Mains, Malerie Marder, Liz Mehl, Jay Nebel, Glenn Patton, Geoff Rickly, Harry Scrymgeour, Cornelius Tittel, Mark Waldron, Ahren Warner, and Maged Zaher.

Love to my family in all its forms including Elizabeth Dickman, Michael Dickman, Jason Van Handel, Wendy Dickman, and the Castelluccis, Huddlestons, Nobles, and Tillinghasts.

The majority of these poems were written during "Poetry Mondays" and with the grace-filled help and encouragement of Major Jackson, Dorianne Laux, Michael McGriff, Joseph Millar, and Sharon Olds.

Deep gratitude to Ray Phelan and Nanette Laufik for being the best neighbors in the world to my sons and me and for keeping a roof over our heads during the first year and beyond of the pandemic.

Thanks to the wonderful Bill Clegg.

Thank you to Drew Elizabeth Weitman and everyone at W. W. Norton & Co.

Immeasurable gratitude to Jill Bialosky, whose continued belief and guidance is both a gift and an honor to receive.

And finally to my sons, Hamza Akalin and Owen Dickman-Tillinghast. I love you.